Little Cells

by Katie McKissick

a Beatrice the Biologist Book

This is a cell.

It is

very small.

Hi!

You have
lots of them.

See your skin?
Those are skin cells.

Your brain
has brain cells.

Your blood has blood cells.

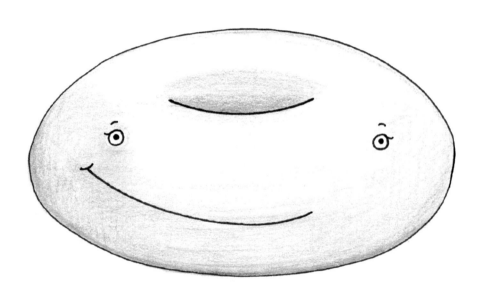

You have
lung cells,

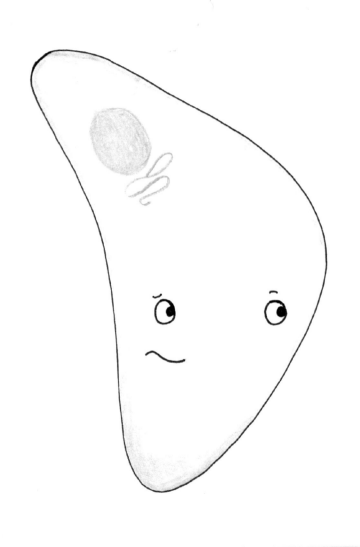

and muscle cells,

and immune cells.

Your cells help you taste,

and smell,

and see.

They make you
who you are.

They are
your cells.

Give them a hug.

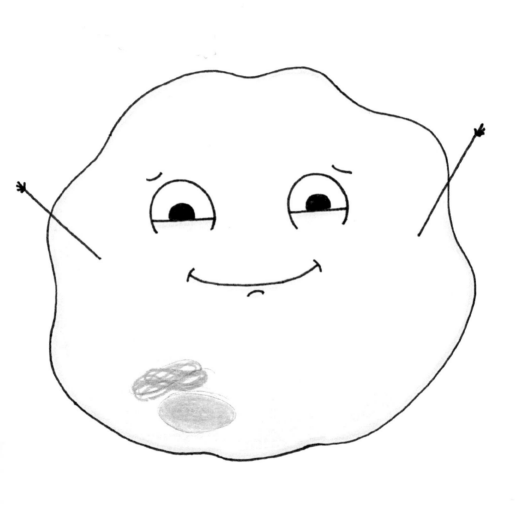

THE END

16190308R10022

Made in the USA
Middletown, DE
08 December 2014